BIG SNACKS, Little Meals

BIG SNACKS, Little Meals

After School, Dinnertime, Anytime

Rose Dunnington

LARK BOOKS
A Division of Sterling Publishing Co., Inc.
New York

Editor
VERONIKA ALICE GUNTER

Creative Director,
Book and Cover Design
CELIA NARANJO

Art Assistant
BRADLEY NORRIS

Photographer
STEVE MANN

Library of Congress Cataloging-in-Publication Data

Dunnington, Rose.
  Big snacks, little meals : after school, dinnertime, anytime / Rose
Dunnington.— 1st ed.
     p. cm.
  Includes index.
  ISBN 1-57990-780-6 (hardcover)
  1. Snack foods. I. Title.
TX740.D866 2006
641.5'3—dc22
                                               2005030429

10 9 8 7 6 5 4 3 2 1

Published by Lark Books, A Division of
Sterling Publishing Co., Inc.
387 Park Avenue South, New York, N.Y. 10016

Text © 2006, Rose Dunnington
Photography © 2006, Lark Books

Distributed in Canada by Sterling Publishing,
c/o Canadian Manda Group, 165 Dufferin Street
Toronto, Ontario, Canada M6K 3H6

Distributed in the United Kingdom by GMC Distribution Services,
Castle Place, 166 High Street, Lewes, East Sussex, England BN7 1XU

Distributed in Australia by Capricorn Link (Australia) Pty Ltd.,
P.O. Box 704, Windsor, NSW 2756 Australia

If you have questions or comments about this book, please contact:
Lark Books
67 Broadway
Asheville, NC 28801
(828) 253-0467

Manufactured in China
All rights reserved

ISBN 13: 978-1-60059-001-6
ISBN 10: 1-60059-001-2

For information about custom editions, special sales, premium and corporate purchases, please
contact Sterling Special Sales Department at 800-805-5489 or specialsales@sterlingpub.com.

This book is dedicated to my brand-new niece,
Caitlyn Eva Dunnington Doughty.
Just wait 'til you get teeth, Cate—
you'll get to chow down on all of this good stuff!

Contents

FEED Yourself!

I was always so hungry when I got off the school bus that I could have eaten Woodrow, our golden retriever.

Luckily for Woodrow, the thought of dog fur in my teeth wasn't particularly appetizing. And luckily for me, I knew how to cook.

I had to cook—my mom refused to buy packaged, ready-to-eat foods. (She thought it was all junk food, and she was mostly right.) So I made omelets, apple pancakes, nachos, and lots of other easy, delicious dishes. The funny thing was, even though they had junk food waiting at home for them, my friends always wanted to come home with me.

Well, finally I figured out why: cooking is almost as fun as eating, and the simple foods my friends and I cooked together tasted amazing. Now you can enjoy making your choice of the 50 great-tasting recipes in this book. They're big snacks and little meals you can whip up anytime a snack attack strikes. You'll get to fool around in the kitchen, try new things, and adjust flavors to get exactly what you're craving.

This is a book about real cooking,

not some little kids' book about making PB&J sandwiches that look like bunnies. You'll start with fresh, basic ingredients, and put them together to make nutritious, substantial dishes. But, believe me, "nutritious" isn't code for "bad tasting." This stuff's super yummy!

Never cooked before? No worries.

Get in the Kitchen!, Are You Ready?, and What's Cooking? tell you everything you need to know to make a sensational snack, from measuring ingredients to mastering basic cooking techniques. Refer to these sections anytime you're not sure what a recipe is telling you to do. If you see an unfamiliar term, look for it in the Glossary beginning on page 110. Words in bold (**like this**) can also be found there. For photographs of cooking equipment, flip to pages 108 and 109.

Real cooking doesn't have to take all day.

These scrumptious recipes go together fast! How fast? Hum-dinger Hummus takes only five minutes, and you can have a Killer Quesadilla in ten. Plan ahead and you'll be able to chill with a Purple Penguin as soon as your book bag hits the floor! If you're not about to faint from hunger, try something more complicated like Awesome Apples or Zucchini Canoes. They take a little extra time to bake, but boy are they worth the wait!

I've organized the recipes according to how you eat them.

By the Handful has mouth-stuffing snacks such as trail mixes that are great on the go. You'll also find seasoned popcorns to munch while you watch a DVD and spiced nuts to boost your brain energy during a study session.

Check out the Finger Lickin' Good recipes for fun hang-out foods. Grab some friends and dig your fingers into an irresistible snack. These are my faves, because, well, I guess I like getting messy. And who can resist sloppy Saucy Drumettes?

Need some knockout good nourishment after soccer practice or when studying runs late? Turn to the Fork It Over chapter for more traditional foods that—surprise—require a fork. But don't worry, there's nothing boring about my Double-Done Potatoes, Mac Attack, and more.

My Lovin' Every Spoonful chapter invites you to dip into yummy food any time of the year, spoon first. Berry Berry Bowl is refreshing in the summer, and Cozy Cocoa Rice Pudding will make you feel comfy and content in the winter.

How do you decide what to make?

Well, different times call for different foods. Whatever your mood or appetite, I've got a recipe to suit it. Want a satisfying snack between meals? Need a quick pick-me-up? Want to surprise your friends with a new taste sensation? You'll find just the right thing on these pages.

Have fun using this book to feed yourself!

Feed Yourself!

Get IN THE KITCHEN!

The kitchen is where you'll make snack magic—as long as you know the difference between boil and broil, and tablespoon and teaspoon. It's easier than it sounds. Just keep reading.

Using a Recipe

My recipes are easy to follow. Just read them all the way through before you start. Each recipe has a title and a tip or story about making or eating the scrumptious snack. I also tell you how much food each recipe makes, such as, "4 to 6 servings." That's the **yield.** I give you a range for the yield because I don't know how hungry you are. You can double or halve a recipe, depending on how many people you want to feed. If you haven't mastered fractions yet, get an adult to check your math.

Ingredients are the foods that you combine to make more delicious food. In this book, ingredients are listed in the order in which you use them, so if you line them up on the counter that way, you won't forget something. The list also tells you how to prepare each ingredient. For instance, you'll see "2 tomatoes, diced," or "1 clove of garlic, minced."

Equipment is what I call the tools you use for cooking. You'll find pictures of basic cooking tools used in this book in the Equipment Glossary on pages 108 and 109.

Instructions tell you, step by step, what to do with the ingredients and equipment. The recipes in this book are easy to prepare, but some of them need extra time to cook or freeze. If you're really hungry, choose something that is ready to eat fast.

The Grocery List

It's frustrating to find a recipe that you want to try and then discover you don't have the ingredients.

Avoid this problem by making a grocery list. Keep a dry-erase board or even just a sheet of paper on the refrigerator, and write down the stuff you need to make your own snacks. When you notice you're getting low on a basic ingredient—like eggs—add it to the list. When you need an ingredient that isn't normally in your kitchen, be specific. If the recipe says, "canned cherries in water or juice," write exactly that on the list.

Measuring

You don't have to measure most ingredients in these recipes exactly. If you really love garlic you can add extra. If you hate it you can leave it out. Recipes that have baking powder, however, should be measured carefully (Puffy Apple Pancake on page 84, for instance).

Most cooking measurements are in volume. Cups, tablespoons, and teaspoons are all measures of volume. You measure liquids in a glass or see-through plastic measuring cup. These usually have tons of lines and numbers; just pour up to the line you want. Measure solid ingredients in scoop-type measuring cups. Sweep the dull edge of a table knife across the rim of the cup for powdery dry ingredients, such as flour. For chunkier things, like diced tomatoes, it's okay if a little bit sticks out of the cup.

Mixing

Putting your measured ingredients together is a common step in recipe instructions. Do you know what each mixing term means?

Combine means to mix the ingredients together just until they're evenly distributed. Do this with a spoon or fork.

Beat means to stir medium fast until the ingredients are a little bit fluffy. Beat with a fork, whisk, or, for quicker results, use an **electric mixer.** Take care when using an electric mixer: dry your hands before you plug or unplug it, and unplug it before you change the attachments or clean it. (To clean a mixer body, wipe it with a wrung-out soapy cloth or sponge.)

Whip means to stir the ingredients very fast until they are super-fluffy. It's hard to get the

Rules, Rules, Rules

Before you start, you'll need to talk with your parents about the rules for using your kitchen. Follow the rules—even if you think they're silly. You'll show your parents that you're trustworthy, which is important.

right consistency with a whisk; use an electric mixer instead.

Blend sometimes means the same thing as combine, but in this book it means that you should use a blender. Make sure your hands are dry before you plug or unplug your blender, and always unplug it before you change the attachments or clean it. (Don't put the base in water when you're cleaning it. You could get an electrical shock and ruin the motor. Just wipe it with a wrung-out sponge.)

Purée means to process food in a blender or **food processor** until the ingredients are soupy.

Pulse means to process the ingredients in a blender or food processor by turning it on and off rhythmically to chop or grind. Most blenders and food processors have a pulse setting.

Toss means to use your hands or **tongs** to lightly mix big pieces of food in spices or sauce until they're coated all over. Don't toss them across the room!

Get in the Kitchen!

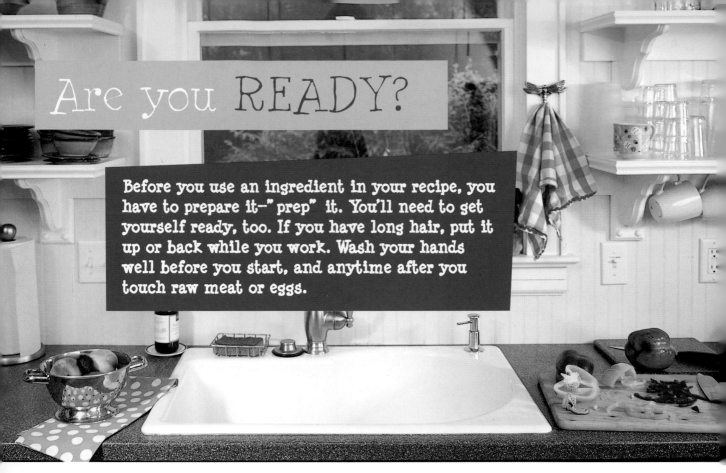

Are you READY?

Before you use an ingredient in your recipe, you have to prepare it—"prep" it. You'll need to get yourself ready, too. If you have long hair, put it up or back while you work. Wash your hands well before you start, and anytime after you touch raw meat or eggs.

Wash all fruits and veggies with plenty of cool running water. If a piece of food feels waxy, use a drop of dish detergent to wash it. Rinse well. Pick out any stems or bad pieces. Okay, you don't have to wash onions, bananas, mangoes, or other foods you peel.

Dry **produce** before you peel or cut it. (It's safer.) Use a peeler, not a knife, to peel most things.

Canned foods require a can opener, and you may need to **drain** or **strain** a canned food by pouring it into a **strainer.** Always strain and rinse beans—that makes them less likely to give you gas.

Using Knives

A knife is like a skateboard—with practice, you can do really cool stuff, but if you aren't careful you'll get hurt. First of all, you need sharp knives. Dull ones are dangerous; they force you to push hard, instead of making easy, controlled cuts. Let an adult check and sharpen your knives. Second, always use a **cutting board.**

There's only one safe way to use a knife. Make a claw out of your **non-dominant** hand, tucking the thumb behind the fingertips. (See the hand position in the slicing and dicing photos on the next page.) Use your claw to hold down the food you'll be cutting. Never raise the knife's blade higher than the knuckles of your guiding hand.

Finally, always take your time and pay attention. If someone starts talking to you while you're using a knife, put it down until you've finished your conversation.

It's a good habit to wash a knife by hand as soon as you've finished using it. NEVER put a knife in a sink of soapy water. It might cut the next person who reaches into the sink. (It's also bad for the knife.)

Cutting Terms

Halving means—you guessed it—cutting an ingredient in half. Place the food on the cutting board and choose a knife that's longer than the food is wide. I use my trusty **chef's knife.** Use one hand to position the blade of the knife on the middle of the food. Bring your other hand over the knife and use the fingers of

that hand on either side of the food to hold it steady. Use a slow, controlled motion to push the knife blade into the food.

Slicing is using one cut to prepare each piece. The thickness of a slice varies according to the recipe. I like bananas for The Bomb on page 74 sliced ¼ inch thick, and tomatoes for Fried Green Tomatoes on page 68 sliced ¾ inch thick. Make slices the same thickness; it looks good and the slices will cook evenly.

Dicing creates cubes of food with all six sides about the same

size. A half inch is a good size. First cut the food into ½-inch thick slices using a chef's knife. Next, cut the food into ½-inch strips. Then give it a quarter turn and cut into ½-inch cubes.

Chopping is sloppy dicing, for when looks aren't important.

Mincing means chopping food into tiny pieces. You usually mince herbs or garlic. To mince, put the food in a low pile on a cutting board, and use a long, sharp knife. Put your guiding hand on top of the knife, and chop, chop, chop. Always keep your guiding hand away from the tip of the knife. Don't put your guiding hand close to the knife's tip. The tip could slip and stab

you. There go your chances of becoming a rock star or a brain surgeon.

Grating creates fine pieces of food, or uniform small chunks of cheese that melt or mix easily. Get a good grip on the food with one hand, and grasp the **grater** with the other. Push the food down at a medium pace along the sharp side of the grate. Graters are just as sharp as knives, so take care

when using them. Use a controlled, careful motion. Don't push as you slide the food back up. A little vegetable oil on a grater keeps cheese from sticking.

13

What's COOKING?

None of the recipes just say, "cook," do they? That's because there are lots of different ways to cook food, and they all give different results.

BAKE. The heat comes from the bottom and fills the whole oven. The goal is to have the same temperature all around the food. Always preheat. Turn on the oven light to check on your food while it cooks. Opening the door lets the heat out.

BROIL. The heat comes from the top of the oven. It's very hot and fast, perfect for Not-Yo Nachos on page 16.

TOASTER OVENS

A **toaster oven** is small and uses less energy than a regular oven. If it does not have a temperature setting, set it on "high" for baking at 375°F or higher, "medium" for 275°F to 375°F, or on "low" for anything below 275°F.

MICROWAVE. Microwaves cook the water inside a food, which is okay for baked potatoes, but makes for really yucky eggs.

SAUTÉ. This means cooking briefly over high heat in oil on the stovetop. Use a **skillet** or a **sauté pan** that's hot. (Flick a drop of water in the skillet; if it sizzles, it's ready for you to add the cooking oil.) Use a skillet big enough so that you have only one layer of food. Stir and flip food, so all sides cook.

BROWN. Browning usually refers to cooking meat or tofu briefly over high heat. It turns brown—of course!

SWEAT. This means cooking ingredients until most of the water has evaporated. The type of pot or pan you use depends on the recipe.

Good Ideas

Keep these tips in mind to turn out terrific snacks—without having to bring out burn ointment and bandages.

• All ovens and stoves are a little bit different. Get an adult to show you how yours work.

• Aim the pan handles to the middle of the stove. That way, they won't be hanging out where you might knock them over. And they won't heat up over another burner, making them too hot to touch.

• Use potholders or oven mitts on both hands to take things out of the oven. Remember: the sides and the door of the oven are hot, too.

• Have a place ready to set hot dishes.

Serving

If you're starving, by all means go ahead and eat! But if you can wait a minute, take the time to make your snack look as good as it tastes. Find the coolest dishes in your cabinets (always ask permission to use extra-fancy ones). Arrange the food to look really appetizing. Eating should be a pleasure for all of your senses!

SIMMER. This is a miniature version of boiling. Tiny bubbles come to the surface of a liquid while it cooks at a steady, medium heat.

BOIL. When a liquid gets hot enough to bubble and turn into steam, it's boiling. Boil in a big pot on the stovetop, filling the pot no more than two-thirds full. Get an adult to move hot, heavy pots for you—grown-ups like to feel useful.

This chapter is full of delicious, eat-with-your-fingers recipes. I call these snacks finger-lickin' good.

This first dish, Not-Yo Nachos, is so good you'll be tempted to not share it.

Not-Yo Nachos

EQUIPMENT

toaster oven (or oven) • measuring cups • baking sheet • chef's knife • cutting board • spoon • grater • potholders

2 TO 4 SERVINGS

- 4 cups tortilla chips
- ½ cup fat-free refried beans
- ½ of a tomato, diced
- ¼ cup sliced pickled banana peppers
- ¼ cup sliced black olives
- 1 cup grated cheddar cheese
- ⅓ cup low-fat sour cream
- ⅓ cup salsa (Try a Sassy Salsa recipe from page 19.)

1. Set the toaster oven to broil. Spread the chips on the baking sheet. Use the spoon to distribute the refried beans, tomatoes, banana peppers, and black olives evenly over the chips. Sprinkle cheese over the whole thing.

2. Broil for 8 to 10 minutes, or until the cheese is melted. Using the potholders, remove the baking sheet from the oven, and carefully slide the nachos onto a plate.

3. Top the nachos with dollops of sour cream and salsa. Dig in.

Sassy Salsas

Sure, you could eat salsa from a jar, but the fresh flavor of homemade salsa explodes in your mouth like the store-bought kind never can. To ensure that none of that flavor explodes in your eyes or other unwelcome places, wash your hands with soap after touching hot peppers.

Classic Salsa

- 2 tomatoes, diced
- ½ medium white onion, diced (you can use 1 scallion, minced, if you prefer a milder flavor)
- 1 jalapeño pepper, minced (optional)
- 1 clove of garlic, minced
- 2 teaspoons vinegar
- 1 teaspoon sugar
- ½ teaspoon salt

Mango Tango

- 2 ripe mangos, diced
- juice of ½ lime
- ½ medium red onion, diced
- ¼ cup cilantro, chopped
- 1 chili pepper minced (optional)
- ½ teaspoon salt

1. For either recipe, combine all ingredients in a mixing bowl or the serving dish. Have a taste and adjust the flavors until they are just right for you.

DICING A MANGO

1. A large, flat pit runs through the center of a mango, so you can't cut it in half the normal way. Instead, cut to either side of the pit. The pit (shown in the lower left corner of the photo) has some good fruit around it, too.

2. Use the table knife to cut a grid pattern in the mango flesh. Then turn the mango half inside out so it looks like a porcupine. See photo. Knock the mango chunks into a mixing bowl or serving dish.

finger-lickin' good

Dip This

EQUIPMENT

measuring cups and spoons • mixing bowl • blender or food processor • chef's knife • cutting board

2 TO 6 SERVINGS

Two secret ingredients—French bread and almonds—make this dip deliciously creamy, without a drop of dairy. Choose a small, medium, or large clove of garlic, depending on just how much you like garlic.

- 4 oz ounces French bread (It's OK if it's stale.)
- cold water
- 1 clove of garlic, peeled
- 1 cup slivered almonds
- 1 teaspoon salt
- 2 tablespoons olive oil
- 1 teaspoon cider vinegar
- pinch of nutmeg
- ¼ cup water (optional)
- raw veggies for dipping

1. Tear the bread into chunks. You should end up with almost 4 cups.

2. Soak the bread in the cold water in the mixing bowl.

3. Puree the garlic with the almonds in the blender until you have a fine paste.

4. Squeeze the water out of the bread, and add the bread to the paste. Add the rest of the ingredients except for the veggies and the optional water, and blend to combine. If you need to, add up to ¼ cup water until you get a good consistency: thick, but not too thick. Dip in with the veggies.

I dipped in with orange and red peppers, plus broccoflower. Have you tried broccoflower? It's green like broccoli, but tastes more like cauliflower.

Benny's Beany Dip

My brother Ben makes this delicious, filling dip for parties. You don't need to save it for a special occasion, but you might enjoy doing a little dance every time you make it.

4 TO 6 SERVINGS

- 1 pound processed cheddar cheese
- 1 can of fat-free refried beans
- 2 cups of salsa
- corn chips for dipping
- diced tomato or pepper for garnish (optional)

1. Cut the cheese into 1-inch chunks. Go ahead and giggle because I said, "cut the cheese."

2. Open the can of beans. Put the cheese, beans, and salsa in the pot. (Ben likes to use a crock-pot.)

3. Cook on medium heat, stirring occasionally, until the cheese is melted and the dip is the same consistency throughout. Transfer the dip to a serving dish if you like.

4. Get down with your bad self!

finger-lickin' good

Stuff It

My friend Andrew had a very sad experience with stuffed mushrooms. He made them to take to a party, but left them on top of his car. They crashed to the ground when he drove away.

EQUIPMENT

toaster oven (or oven) • clean kitchen towel • mixing bowl • greased baking sheet • measuring cups and spoons • chef's knife • cutting board • nonstick skillet • stove • wooden spoon • grater • potholders

2 TO 5 SERVINGS

- 8-ounce package of button, crimini, or baby bella mushrooms (Crimini and baby bella are actually the same thing.)
- 2 tablespoons olive oil
- salt and pepper
- cooking spray
- 1 clove garlic, minced
- 2/3 cup stuffing mix or bread crumbs
- 1/3 cup parmesan cheese, grated
- 1 teaspoon minced sage

1. Preheat the toaster oven to 350°F. With the clean kitchen towel, wipe off as much dirt as you can from the mushrooms. Quickly rinse the rest of the dirt off under running water. (Mushrooms absorb water fast, so wash them quickly.)

2. Gently wiggle the stems out of the mushroom caps. Mince the stems only. Save for later.

3. Toss the mushroom caps with 1 tablespoon of the olive oil and a pinch each of salt and pepper in the mixing bowl. Arrange the mushroom caps on the baking sheet hollow sides up.

4. After heating the remaining tablespoon of olive oil in the skillet on medium-high heat, sauté the garlic and mushroom stems for 5 to 7 minutes. Stir with the wooden spoon until most of the juice has evaporated.

5. Transfer the garlic and mushroom stems to the mixing bowl. Add the stuffing mix or bread crumbs, cheese, and sage. Stir. Add a pinch or two of salt and pepper if you like, and then spoon the filling into the mushroom caps. Bake for 10 to 12 minutes.

6. After using your potholders to take the sheet out of the oven, let the mushrooms cool before you pop one in your mouth.

Pear-fection

Blue cheese and pears are the perfect flavor pair, and walnuts add crunch. If blue cheese is too stinky for you, substitute 1 heaping tablespoon of strawberry jam. But don't write-off blue cheese forever. Taste buds change, so give it another try in a few years.

- 1 pear, washed, dried, and cored (See how to core on page 73.)
- ¼ cup low-fat cream cheese, softened to room temperature
- ¼ cup crumbled blue cheese
- ½ teaspoon milk
- handful of walnuts, chopped

EQUIPMENT

apple corer • chef's knife • cutting board • measuring cups and spoons • mixing bowl • spoon

2 TO 4 SERVINGS

1. Use the knife to slice the cored pear on the cutting board into disks about ¼ inch thick.

2. Combine the cheeses and the milk in the mixing bowl. Stir with the spoon until well blended. Spread the mixture on the pear slices.

3. Sprinkle the walnuts on top of the cheese.

finger-lickin' good

Hum-Dinger Hummus

People have been enjoying hummus snacks for thousands of years. You can taste for yourself why it hasn't gotten old yet. Scoop the hummus to your mouth with pita bread, olives, cucumber sticks, or carrot sticks.

EQUIPMENT

can opener • strainer • blender or food processor • chef's knife • cutting board • blender or food • processor • rubber spatula • vegetable peeler

2 TO 4 SERVINGS

- 1 15 oz. can garbanzo beans (also called chickpeas)
- 1 clove of garlic, peeled
- 3 tablespoons tahini (You can find this sesame seed paste with international foods or peanut butter, depending on the grocery store.)
- 1 tablespoon olive oil
- salt
- 1 lemon, halved
- water (optional)
- paprika (optional)
- 2 pieces of pita bread cut into wedges (optional)
- 1 medium cucumber, peeled and cut into sticks (optional)
- 2 medium carrots, peeled and cut into sticks (optional)

1. Open the can of garbanzo beans. Strain the juice, and rinse the beans with fresh water. Put the beans into the blender.

2. Add the garlic, tahini, olive oil, and salt to the blender or food processor. Next, squeeze the juice from the lemon into the blender. (A good trick is to hold your hand over the blender, and let the juice dribble between your fingers so you catch the seeds, or you can use a strainer.)

3. Put the lid on the blender, and blend away! You're going for a smooth mush. If you need to, stop the blender, and use the rubber spatula to push the ingredients off of the sides and into the center.

4. If the mixture is too stiff, blend in a little water to thin it out.

5. Scrape the hummus with the rubber spatula into a serving dish. You can sprinkle a little paprika on top. It looks cool and tastes great.

Heavenly Eggs

These are usually called "deviled eggs," but they taste divine. In cooking, "deviled" means the food is combined with something spicy (in this case mustard) to make it tangy. There's also deviled ham, but I've never tried that. Have you?

- 6 eggs
- water
- 2 tablespoons mayonnaise
- 2 tablespoons mustard
- 2 tablespoons pickle relish (sweet or dill, your choice)
- salt and pepper to taste
- paprika (optional)

Certified cage-free or free-range chickens have happier lives than conventionally farmed chickens. Their eggs taste better too.

1. Carefully make a tiny hole in the skinny end of each egg with the push pin. (This keeps the eggs from cracking when they boil.) Then put the eggs in the pot, and fill it halfway with the water.

2. Bring the water to a boil on high heat, and then turn the stove off right away. Set the timer for 11 minutes. While you're waiting, you can always rock out to your favorite CD—just don't play it too loud, or you won't hear the timer!

3. Use the slotted spoon to scoop the eggs out of the hot water and into the mixing bowl. Run cool water over them until they're comfortable to handle.

4. Roll each egg on the cutting board to crack the shell, and peel the shells off (my favorite part!). Make sure you clear all the little pieces of eggshell out of your work area, so they don't accidentally end up in the food. Dump the water out of the mixing bowl.

5. Use the knife and the cutting board to cut each egg in half lengthwise, and then use the spoon to scoop the yolks into the mixing bowl. Set the egg whites aside.

6. Now add the mayonnaise, mustard, and pickle relish to the yokes. Mash and stir with the fork until you have a fluffy mixture. Then add salt and pepper to taste.

7. Spoon the filling back into the egg whites. Sprinkle paprika on the deviled eggs if you like the way it looks.

finger-lickin' good

Pineapple Pumpernickel Pinwheels

If you want really pretty pinwheels, use big slices of bread. Grapes and walnuts on the side turn this snack into a meal.

EQUIPMENT

can opener • small mixing bowl • fork • table knife • cutting board • knife • toothpicks

2 TO 3 SERVINGS (12 WHEELS)

- 2 tablespoons crushed pineapple in juice, drained
- ¼ cup low-fat cream cheese, softened to room temperature
- 2 slices of pumpernickel bread

1. Combine the pineapple and cream cheese in the small mixing bowl with the fork.

2. Use the table knife to spread some of the filling on a bread slice, roll it up lengthwise, and cut the roll into rounds with the knife on the cutting board. Secure each round with a toothpick. Do the same thing with the rest of the bread and filling.

Brain Freeze

Frozen pops are the ultimate chill out. If you don't have freezer molds, use 3-ounce paper cups. Cover filled paper cups with aluminum foil, then poke the stick through.

EQUIPMENT

measuring cups • colander • cutting board • blender or food processor • 6 to 8 freezer molds or 6 to 8 paper cups • 6 to 8 craft sticks or plastic spoons (optional) • bowl or pot

6 TO 8 POPS

Purple Penguins

- 2 cups blueberries, rinsed and picked
- 2 cups low-fat vanilla yogurt
- 1 cup powdered sugar

1. Combine the blueberries, yogurt, and sugar in the blender and blend like crazy. Really. Blend a whole lot—longer than it looks like you need to—or you'll get unpleasant, grainy bits of peel and seed in the finished pop.
2. Pour the mixture into the freezer molds, leaving at least ½ inch empty at the top because liquids expand when they freeze.
3. Freeze for 2 hours, or until solid. (It will all depend on how fast your freezer works.)
4. To unmold, fill the bowl or pot with the hot water, and dip the molds in it until you can wiggle the pops out by their handles. If you're using paper cups, just tear the paper away.

Orange You Glad It's Summer?

- 6 oranges, halved (Fresh-squeezed juice is what makes these pops delicious.)
- 8-ounce can crushed pineapple in juice
- ¼ cup honey

1. Squeeze the juice from the oranges into a mixing bowl and fish out the seeds. Mix in the other ingredients—pineapple juice included. Then follow steps 2, 3, and 4 from the instructions above.

Watermelon Wowzers

- small watermelon, or ¼ of a large one

1. Cut the watermelon's soft insides into chunks and remove the seeds with your fingers. Stuff the chunks in the molds and stab them with a fork until they've released enough juice to fill in the gaps. Finish by following steps 3 and 4 above.

finger-lickin' good

PB&J Ice Cream Sandwiches

EQUIPMENT

spoon • mixing bowl • measuring cups • rubber spatula • baking dish, 9-inch square • waxed paper • freezer • chef's knife • cutting board • table knife • plastic wrap and resealable freezer bag (optional)

9 SANDWICHES

Here's a new twist on a classic snack. Get a friend or two to help put them together so the PB part doesn't melt until it's in your mouths. Of course, if you're working alone you can just stick the ice cream back in the freezer for a couple of minutes if it gets too soft.

- 1 pint regular or low-fat vanilla ice cream
- ½ cup peanut butter (creamy or crunchy—you choose)
- 9 full-size graham crackers
- ¼ cup of your favorite jam or jelly

1. Spoon the ice cream into the mixing bowl. Soften it by leaving the ice cream out on the counter for 10 minutes.

2. Mix the peanut butter into the ice cream with the rubber spatula.

3. Line the baking dish with waxed paper and spread the peanut butter-ice cream mixture on the waxed paper. Cover the mixture with another sheet of waxed paper, and then put the mixture in the freezer for 20 to 45 minutes, or until solid.

4. Turn the frozen mixture out onto the cutting board, and peel off the waxed paper. Use the chef's knife to cut the mixture into nine squares the same size as the graham crackers you're using.

5. With the table knife, spread the jam or jelly on a graham cracker, add a square of peanut butter-ice cream mixture, and top with another graham cracker. Put each finished sandwich in the freezer immediately, so it doesn't melt before you've made them all. You can also wrap each PB&J Ice Cream Sandwich in plastic wrap and store them in a freezer bag in the freezer.

Jigglers

EQUIPMENT

measuring cup • mixing bowl • sauce pot • stove • spoon • shallow baking dish • refrigerator • table knife or cookie cutters

4 TO 6 SERVINGS

- 4 cups cold fruit juice (Don't use pineapple or papaya—they contain an enzyme that breaks down gelatin.)
- 3 tablespoons unflavored gelatin

1. Pour 1 cup of cold juice into the mixing bowl, and sprinkle the gelatin on it. Let it sit until the gelatin absorbs the liquid. (This is called blooming.)

2. Pour the remaining 3 cups of juice into the sauce pot, and heat on medium until it's the same temperature as a nice warm bath.

3. Pour the warm juice into the mixing bowl, and stir with the spoon until the gelatin dissolves.

4. Pour the mixture into the baking dish. The gelatin should be no more than 1 inch deep if you're going to cut the jigglers with the cookie cutters.

5. Refrigerate for 3 to 5 hours until it's solid.

6. Cut the jigglers any shape you like. Serve and eat.

finger-lickin' good

The Real Deal Tacos

EQUIPMENT

measuring cups and spoons •
2 skillets • stove • chef's
knife • cutting board •
wooden spoon • tongs

3 TACOS

These may not be the kind of tacos you're used to, but I think they're the best. Plus they're a good way to turn boring leftovers into something new. These can be drippy, so make sure you've got plenty of napkins.

- about 1 tablespoon cooking oil (I use olive oil.)
- 1 cup chopped cooked meat (chicken, pork or beef leftovers work well)
- 1 clove garlic, peeled and minced
- 1/4 teaspoon chili powder
- 6 corn tortillas (Get the floppy, beige kind, not the crunchy, yellow kind.)
- 1/2 of a small sweet white onion, diced
- 1/3 cup chopped cilantro
- 1/4 cup salsa verde (sometimes labeled green salsa for people who don't know that verde means green in Spanish)
- 1 lime, cut into wedges

1. Put enough oil in one of the skillets to lightly cover the bottom. Heat the pan on medium heat.

2. Add the meat and the garlic to the pan. You want it to heat through, so stir it occasionally with the wooden spoon while you're doing the rest of the stuff.

3. Rub a little bit of the oil on both sides of your tortillas. (You will need two tortillas for each taco.)

4. Put the other skillet on the stove, and turn the heat to medium high. Use the tongs to put the tortillas into the pan, and cook them one at a time for about 30 seconds on each side.

5. Now it's time to put the tacos together. First take 2 tortillas, and then spoon on a little meat, a sprinkle of the onions and cilantro, a spoonful of the salsa verde, and a squirt of the lime. Delicioso!

Can you substitute squash for the meat? Of course you can! Cooking is all about creativity – and making something that tastes good to you. Just think what a sad world we would live in if no one had experimented with adding sugar to chocolate!

Chicken Fingers

Chickens don't have fingers! I think the name comes from how you eat them. This part of the chicken is the loin, which comes from the breast. The loin has a little yellowish-white tendon at one end that is sometimes tough to chew. You can cut this tendon off after you wash and dry the meat, but I usually leave it on. Hey, I'm lazy!

- 1 pound chicken tenders (The package might call them "loins.")
- 1 cup flour
- 1 teaspoon salt
- $\frac{1}{2}$ teaspoon pepper
- $\frac{1}{4}$ teaspoon baking powder
- 1 egg
- cooking spray (known as "spray grease" at my house)
- Honey Baby Sauce (See recipe below.)

Honey Baby Sauce

Combine $\frac{1}{4}$ cup honey with $\frac{1}{4}$ cup spicy brown mustard in a small bowl.

If you're sharing, let each person have their own little bowl of sauce.

1. Preheat the toaster oven to 375°F. Rinse the chicken under running water in the colander, and blot it dry with the paper towels. The drying part is important because the coating won't stick to wet chicken, so don't skip it.

2. Combine the dry ingredients in one of the shallow dishes. (Since this recipe uses baking powder, you need to measure out the dry ingredients carefully.) Use the fork to mix them together.

3. Use the fork to beat the egg lightly in the other shallow dish. Now the fun part: **dredge** each piece of chicken first in the flour (shake off any extra), then in the egg, and then back in the flour. See photo.  Finally, place the chicken on the baking sheet. Lightly spray the tops of the dredged chicken with oil.

4. Bake for 15 minutes. Flip the chicken pieces over with the tongs. Lightly spray them with oil, and bake another 5 minutes until golden brown.

5. Let the chicken fingers cool before you dip them in Honey Baby Sauce. Chow down.

finger-lickin' good

Saucy Drumettes

I prefer the part of the chicken wing that looks like a miniature drumstick to the part with two bones, so that's how I wrote the recipe. But you can use both if that's what you like—just make sure the wings are precut. Serve this saucy snack with celery sticks and ranch or blue cheese dressing.

EQUIPMENT

oven • paper towels • 2 mixing bowls • greased baking sheet • potholders • tongs

3 TO 6 SERVINGS

- 1 pound chicken drumettes (A drumette is part of a chicken's wing.)
- cooking spray
- sauce of your choice (Use one of these four.)

Classic Buffalo Sauce

- ¼ cup butter
- ¾ cup hot pepper sauce
- 1½ teaspoons cornstarch

1. Choose and make one of the sauces below. For Classic Buffalo Sauce, whisk the cornstarch and hot sauce together in a small sauce pot until smooth. Add the butter, and heat over a medium burner until the butter is melted. Cook and stir an additional 3 to 5 minutes until the sauce thickens. For the other sauces, just combine the ingredients in a bowl. Divide the sauce between two bowls—one for raw chicken and one for cooked.

2. Preheat the oven to 375°F. Rinse the chicken drumettes, and blot them dry with the paper towels.

3. Toss the drumettes with the tongs in the bowl with half of the sauce you made. Then spread the drumettes in an even layer on the baking sheet, and bake for 40 to 45 minutes. Wash your hands and the tongs.

4. After taking the sheet out of the oven (use your potholders), use the tongs to toss the drumettes in the remaining sauce. Let them cool before scarfing them down.

Sesame Ginger

- ¼ cup white vinegar
- ½ cup honey
- 1 tablespoon soy sauce
- 4 teaspoons toasted sesame oil
- 2 teaspoons powdered ginger
- ½ teaspoon garlic powder
- 1 tablespoon sesame seeds (I used black ones.)

BBQ Sauce

- ¼ cup white vinegar
- ½ cup ketchup
- ¼ cup brown sugar
- ½ teaspoon salt
- ¼ teaspoon pepper
- ½ teaspoon Worcestershire sauce
- ¼ teaspoon garlic powder

Not-Your-Honey Mustard

- ¼ cup white vinegar
- ⅓ cup honey
- ¼ cup prepared mustard
- 2 tablespoons dry mustard
- ¼ teaspoon salt

Burritos Muy Buenos

I can't explain why, but these "very good burritos" sound even better in Spanish. If you prepare the fillings ahead of time and store them in the refrigerator, you can whip up one of these wraps in no time.

EQUIPMENT

measuring cups and spoons • chef's knife • cutting board • skillet • stove • wooden spoon • can opener • strainer • table knife • microwave • grater

4 BIG BURRITOS

- 1 tablespoon olive oil
- 1 small onion, diced
- 16-ounce can of black beans, drained and rinsed
- 1 bay leaf
- ¾ teaspoon chili powder
- ¾ teaspoon salt
- 1 avocado
- 4 flour tortillas
- 1⅓ cup of your favorite kind of grated cheese (I like to blend cheddar and Monterey Jack.)
- 1 tomato, diced
- 2 cups cooked rice (Just follow the package directions if you don't have leftover rice.)
- 1 cup salsa (You can either get it from a jar, or try a Sassy Salsa recipe from page 18.)

1. Heat the olive oil in the skillet on medium heat until the oil shimmers. Then sauté the onion in the oil, stirring with the wooden spoon until you can almost see through the onions.

2. Add the beans, bay leaf, chili powder, and salt to the onions. Use the wooden spoon to combine the ingredients. Let them heat up while you prepare the rest of the food.

3. Halve the avocado, twisting the halves apart to remove the pit. Hold the avocado on the cutting board and use the table knife to cut a grid in the avocado's insides. Scoop the chunks out with a spoon. See photo.

4. Microwave the tortillas for 20 seconds, to make them easy to fold. Lay them on a plate, and then use the spoon to put one-fourth of the cheese, tomatoes, rice, salsa, and bean-and-onion mixture into a tortilla. Sprinkle on the avocado pieces.

5. Fold the top and bottom of the tortilla over the filling. Then fold one side over, and roll the burrito up. Repeat for the other three tortillas.

finger-lickin' good

Shrimply Scrumptious

If you haven't had shrimp this way before, you should know that the tails are left on just so you can use them as handles. Then it's easy to dip the meat into a yummy sauce. I ate a shrimp tail once, and I don't recommend it.

2 SERVINGS

- ½ pound easy-peel raw shrimp (in your grocery's seafood section)
- 2 teaspoons olive oil
- ¼ teaspoon salt
- ¼ teaspoon pepper

1. Preheat the oven to 450°F. Rinse the shrimp in the colander under cool running water.
2. Use your clean fingers to peel the shell and legs off of the shrimp, but leave the tails on. Blot the shrimp dry on paper towels.
3. Toss all of the ingredients together in the mixing bowl so that shrimp are coated. Then spread the shrimp in a single layer on the baking sheet.
4. Bake for 5 to 7 minutes, or until the shrimp are solid and bright pink. Use your potholders when you take the sheet out of the oven.

Kooky Cocktail Sauce

- 2 tablespoons ketchup
- 2 teaspoons prepared horseradish
- 1 teaspoon lemon juice
- ⅛ teaspoon salt

1. For both of these easy sauces, just combine all ingredients in a small bowl. Transfer to a fancy serving dish if you'd like.
2. Dip in!

Tempt-Me Tahini Dip

- juice of 1 lime
- 1 tablespoon grated fresh ginger
- ¼ cup low-fat mayonnaise
- ¼ cup tahini (Find it near the international foods or peanut butter in your grocery store.)
- 1 tablespoon soy sauce
- 1 tablespoon rice vinegar (or white wine vinegar)
- 1 tablespoon sesame oil

Killer Quesadillas

My husband is nicknamed Stevie Quesadilla because this is his favorite snack. I serve it with my Holy Moly Guacamole.

1 TO 4 SERVINGS (1 QUESADILLA)

- 1 teaspoon butter
- 1 flour tortilla
- 2 ounces cheddar, mozzarella, or Monterey jack cheese (or a combination), grated

Optional tasty ingredients:
- sliced tomato
- browned meat or tofu
- chopped scallions
- diced avocado (See page 47.)
- sprouts
- guacamole (See recipe below.)
- diced bell pepper

1. Melt the butter in the skillet on medium heat.

2. Put the tortilla in the pan. Next, put the cheese and, if you like, a filling or two on half of the tortilla. Use the spatula to fold the other side of the tortilla over the fillings.

3. Cook for 2 to 3 minutes. Flip the quesadilla over, and cook 2 to 3 minutes more. Let the cheese cool for a minute before you take a bite. Put a little guacamole on top for extra flavor.

When I was a kid I said I didn't want to eat guacamole. My papa said, "Fine. More for me." That made me suspicious, so I tried a nibble. Then I took a bite. Then I scooped a huge mound of it on a chip and rammed it into my mouth. It was the best stuff I'd ever eaten. Here's my recipe.

Holy Moly Guacamole

- 1 avocado
- ¼ teaspoon salt
- 1 small clove of garlic, peeled and minced
- juice of 1 lime

1. Mash the insides of the avocado with the salt, garlic, and lime juice. (To see how to get to the insides of an avocado, see page 47, but you can skip the grid part for this recipe.)

2. If you like, add diced onion, chopped tomato or cilantro, or cayenne pepper to taste.

3. Wrap and refrigerate leftovers immediately, or they'll turn brown.

finger-lickin' good

Sometimes you want to dig in with your whole hand and fill your mouth with something crunchy and full of interesting flavors.

Be careful: the snacks in this chapter—like these crispy, spicy nuts—could be habit-forming.

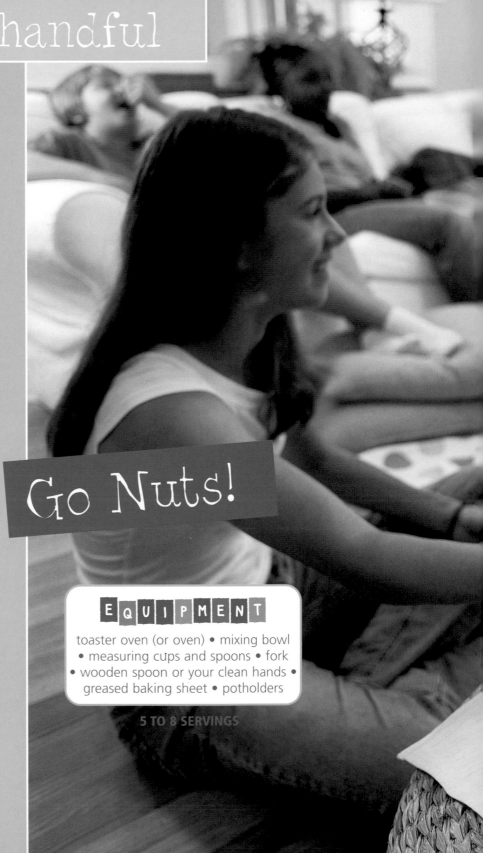

Go Nuts!

EQUIPMENT

toaster oven (or oven) • mixing bowl • measuring cups and spoons • fork • wooden spoon or your clean hands • greased baking sheet • potholders

5 TO 8 SERVINGS

- 1 egg white
- ½ cup sugar
- ¼ teaspoon cinnamon
- ½ teaspoon chili powder
- 2 cups salted mixed nuts

1. Preheat the oven to 350°F.

2. Separate the egg white. Here's how: gently crack the egg on the side of the mixing bowl; hold the egg over the bowl as you carefully slide the yolk back and forth between each half shell; meanwhile, the egg white falls into the bowl. Discard the yolk and shell.

3. Add the sugar and spices to the egg white, and then it beat with the fork.

4. Use the wooden spoon or your clean hands to toss the nuts with the egg mixture until they are evenly coated.

5. Spread the nuts on the baking sheet. Bake for 10 minutes. Stir and bake for 5 more minutes.

Pop Pop Pop

ONE BIG, TASTY BOWLFUL

Way back in the dark ages, before there was microwave popcorn, we popped corn on the stovetop. Have you ever done it this way? It's pretty neat, and the best part is that you get to add exactly the flavorings you want.

- cooking oil (I use olive oil.)
- popcorn kernels
- seasoning mix of your choice (See below.)

Go Italian

- a handful of grated parmesan cheese
- a sprinkle of garlic powder
- a sprinkle of mixed Italian herbs

Sugar & Spice

- a spoonful of sugar
- a shake of ground cinnamon
- a sprinkle of salt

Spice It Up

- a shake of cayenne pepper
- a sprinkle of garlic powder
- a shake of celery salt
- a dash of salt

1. Pour enough oil into the pot to coat the bottom and heat on medium-high heat until the oil shimmers. That means it's hot enough to pop your kernels.

2. Add enough popcorn kernels to make a single layer on the bottom of the pot. Reduce the heat to medium, and put the lid on the pot. When you hear the kernels start to pop, hold on to the handles (use the potholders), and shake the pot over the heat source while the popcorn pops.

3. When the popping slows down to the point that you don't hear a pop for 10 seconds, take the pot off of the burner, and turn off the stove. Don't worry if you hear a few more pops coming from the pot.

4. Take off the lid, and dump the popcorn into the serving bowl. (This can be exciting if there are a few late poppers.) If your pot's really heavy, get an adult to dump it for you. Sprinkle a seasoning mix on the popcorn, and toss it with your hands.

Double Feature

- a handful of peanuts
- a handful of chocolate candies
- a sprinkle of salt

You'll Be My BFF

- a sprinkle of nutritional yeast (found at health food stores)
- a dash of salt

Caramel Corn

Here's a great crunchy, munchy accompaniment for your favorite DVD. I like to change into my jammies, pour some juice, and cozy up with lots of pillows to watch a movie. And I have to put on my glasses. If you wear glasses too, avoid touching them with greasy popcorn fingers, or you'll have to pause the movie to clean your glasses. This gives everyone else a chance to polish off the caramel corn while you're not looking!

EQUIPMENT

4-quart pot with lid • stove • potholders • serving bowl • measuring spoons • sauce pot • wooden spoon

ONE BIG BOWL

- cooking oil
- popcorn kernels
- 2 tablespoons butter
- 1 cup brown sugar

1. Pop the popcorn. See Pop Pop Pop on page 54 if you need instructions.

2. Prepare the caramel. Just combine the butter and the brown sugar in the saucepot on medium-high heat, stirring occasionally until the mixture boils. Turn off the stove and remove the saucepot from the heat.

3. Dump the popped corn into the serving bowl. Drizzle the caramel mixture over the popcorn. See photo. Mix it up with the wooden spoon instead of with your hands because it's hot. Make sure to let your Caramel Corn cool off before you eat it.

by the handful

Trail Mixes

Some people call Keep on Truckin' GORP, which is an acronym for "good ol' raisins and peanuts." I added some good ol' chocolate to my recipe. Take some with you for a snack anytime you might need a quick energy boost. Like for soccer practice, ballet class, or walrus juggling.

Keep on Truckin'

- ½ cup raisins
- ¾ cup salted peanuts
- ¼ cup chocolate candies

1. Use your clean, dry hands to mix the ingredients in the bowl. If you want to take this snack with you or save some for later, put a few handfuls of the trail in a resealable plastic bag. Store it in a cool, dry place. (Not in the refrigerator.)

Spring Break

- ½ cup dried pineapple chunks
- ½ cup banana chips
- ½ cup shredded coconut
- ½ cup salted cashews
- ¼ cup white chocolate chips

Bear Food

- ½ cup dried apple pieces
- ¼ cup dried cranberries
- ½ cup walnuts
- ½ cup mini pretzels

Don't feed the bears!
Eat it yourself.

Scrum-diddly-umptious

You'll need a cutting board and knife.
- ¼ cup chopped dried apricots
- ¼ cup candied ginger
- 1 cup almonds
- ¼ cup shredded coconut
- ¼ cup chocolate chips

Roasty-Toasty

Have you ever carved a jack-o'-lantern? Did you know there were ingredients for a tasty snack inside? Just separate the seeds from the stringy glop, and then rinse and dry the seeds before using them. You can also buy raw pumpkin seeds in bulk at some grocery stores.

- 1 cup pumpkin seeds, rinsed and dried
- ½ teaspoon salt
- ¼ teaspoon chili powder (optional)

1. Preheat the oven to 450°F. Spread the seeds in an even layer on the baking sheet, and bake for 2 to 3 minutes.

2. Wear your potholders to take the sheet out of the oven, and then use the spatula to help slide the roasted seeds into the serving bowl.

3. Toss the seeds with the salt (and chili powder if you like things spicy). Munch.

My papa uses a different method to roast pumpkin seeds. He heats about a teaspoon of olive oil in a skillet and sautés the seeds on the stove over medium heat, stirring occasionally. You can do it either way.

by the handful

Instant Party Mix

This nut mix is so delicious, you should invite a couple of your best friends over to share. The result? Instant party.

4 TO 6 SERVINGS

- 3 tablespoons butter or margarine
- ½ teaspoon garlic powder
- ½ teaspoon salt
- ½ teaspoon paprika
- 1 tablespoon Worcestershire sauce
- 1 cup minipretzel rods
- 1 cup rice cereal
- 1 cup corn cereal
- 1 cup wheat cereal
- 1 cup mixed nuts

1. Preheat the oven to 275°. Melt the butter directly on the baking sheet in the oven while it's preheating.

2. Using the potholders, slide the sheet out of the oven, and use the spatula to stir the seasonings into the melted butter.

3. Add everything else, and carefully stir to coat all the dry ingredients with the butter and seasonings.

4. Bake for 20 minutes. Again, using the potholders, slide the sheet out of the oven, and stir the mix around. Then bake for 10 more minutes.

Looking for easy recipes guaranteed to satisfy your empty stomach? You've found them here in Fork it Over.

To start off, use spaghetti left over from last night's dinner to make this pie that tastes a lot like lasagna.

Spaghetti Pie

EQUIPMENT

oven • wooden spoon • mixing bowl • microwave • measuring cups and spoons • greased pie plate • grater • potholders

4 TO 6 SERVINGS

- 15-ounce container of ricotta cheese
- 1 egg
- 1 cup marinara sauce
- 10-ounce package frozen spinach
- 4 cups cooked spaghetti
- ½ teaspoon basil
- ½ teaspoon oregano
- ½ teaspoon salt
- ½ teaspoon pepper
- 2 ounces mozzarella cheese, grated

1. Preheat the oven to 375°F. Crack the egg into the mixing bowl and discard the shell. Add the ricotta cheese and the marinara sauce to the bowl and use the wooden spoon to combine them with the egg.

2. After thawing the spinach in the microwave (follow the package instructions), squeeze the water out of the spinach, and add the spinach to the bowl.

3. Add the spaghetti, basil, oregano, salt, and pepper. Stir with the wooden spoon until well combined, and transfer to the greased pie plate. Sprinkle the mozzarella on top.

4. Bake for 25 to 30 minutes, until the cheese melts and starts to brown. Remember to use your potholders when taking the pie out of the oven. Let it cool a bit and transfer each serving onto a plate before you dig in.

Super-Fly Pad Thai

I've simplified one of my favorite dishes so you can make it fast. If you want, you can add cooked shrimp, chicken, or tofu. If you don't like spicy food, skip the red pepper flakes.

2 OR 3 SERVINGS

- 4 ounces wide rice noodles (sold with the Asian foods at the grocery store or at an Asian market)
- hot water
- 1 lime, halved
- 2 tablespoons fish sauce (sold with the Asian foods at the grocery store)
- 1 teaspoon garlic powder
- pinch of red pepper flakes (optional)
- 1½ teaspoons soy sauce
- 2 tablespoons sugar
- 1 tablespoon peanut oil
- ¼ cup cilantro, chopped
- 1 egg
- ¼ cup unsalted peanuts (If you use salted peanuts, reduce the soy sauce to 1 teaspoon.)
- 1 cup bean sprouts

1. Soak the noodles in hot water in the medium mixing bowl while you make the sauce and scramble the egg.

2. Squeeze the juice from the lime into a small mixing bowl. Dig out any seeds with your fingers and discard the seeds. Add the fish sauce, garlic powder, red pepper flakes, soy sauce, sugar, and peanut oil to the lime juice. Beat with the fork to combine.

3. Scramble the egg in the skillet over medium heat. Have you scrambled an egg before? Just crack the egg into the heated nonstick skillet and stir with a heatproof rubber spatula to break up the chunks while it cooks. When the eggs are solid, drain the water off of the noodles and add them to the skillet.

4. Add the sauce, the peanuts, and the bean sprouts to the skillet. Stir everything together with the tongs, and cook until it's all warm.

5. Turn off the stove, take the skillet off the burner, and transfer your Super-Fly Pad Thai to serving plates with tongs. Sprinkle cilantro on top of each serving and try eating with chopsticks.

Fried Green Tomatoes

E Q U I P M E N T

measuring spoons • 3 shallow dishes
(pie plates work well) • fork • skillet •
stove • chef's knife • cutting board •
spatula (for flipping)

2 SERVINGS

Did you know that tomatoes are delicious even before they're ripe? If your grocery store doesn't carry green tomatoes, find someone with a garden. I think a fair trade would be 5 minutes of weeding for 1 tomato. If you double this recipe, don't double the egg or hot pepper sauce.

- 2 tablespoons flour
- 1 egg
- ¼ teaspoon hot pepper sauce
- 3 tablespoons yellow cornmeal
- ¼ teaspoon salt
- ½ teaspoon dill
- 2 tablespoons cooking oil
- 1 medium-sized green tomato, cut into slices about ½ inch thick

1. Put the flour in the first shallow dish. Lightly beat the egg and the hot pepper sauce in the second dish, and stir togther the cornmeal, salt, and dill in the third.

2. Heat the cooking oil in the skillet on medium. You'll know it's hot enough to start cooking if you flick a drop into the pan and the water sizzles.

3. **Dredge** each tomato slice in the flour (knock off any extra), then in the egg, then finally in the corn-meal mixture. (See page 43 for a picture of my friend Marcus dredging chicken.)

4. Carefully transfer the slices to the skillet with the spatula. (Be careful not to touch the pan. I don't want you to burn yourself.) Sauté for 3 minutes on each side. Remove from the skillet with the spatula.

Zucchini Canoes

Have a little luau! The zucchini is juicy and crunchy, but most of the flavor in the dish comes from the Hawaiian-inspired filling. Trust me, one bite, and you'll be doing the hula.

E Q U I P M E N T

toaster oven (or oven) • chef's knife • cutting board • spoon • baking sheet • wooden spoon • can opener (optional) • measuring spoons and cups • mixing bowl • grater • potholders

4 CANOES

- 2 medium-sized zucchinis, halved lengthwise
- ½ teaspoon vegetable oil
- 2 slices deli ham, chopped into bite-sized pieces
- ½ cup stuffing mix
- ¼ cup canned chunks pineapple, drained, or fresh pineapple, diced
- ¼ cup marinara sauce
- ½ cup grated mozzarella cheese

1. Preheat the oven to 375°F or the high setting. Scrape the seeds out of the zucchinis with the spoon. See photo.

2. Rub a little bit of the vegetable oil on the outsides of the zucchinis, and place them skin side down on the baking sheet.

3. Use the wooden spoon to combine the ham, the stuffing mix, the pineapple, and the marinara sauce in the mixing bowl. Stir it up.

4. Spoon the filling into the hollowed-out zucchinis. Sprinkle the cheese on top of the filling, and bake for 20 for 25 minutes. Be sure to use your potholders when you take the sheet out of the oven.

Awesome Apples

You could eat one of these apples for an afternoon snack and save the rest for your family's dessert. Ah yes, you are talented, generous, kind, and sweet. Bask in your well-deserved praise.

6 SERVINGS

- 6 medium-sized apples (Granny Smith apples work well)
- ¼ cup softened butter
- ½ cup quick oats
- ½ cup brown sugar
- 1 tablespoon flour
- 1 teaspoon cinnamon
- ½ cup pecans
- ½ cup raisins
- vanilla ice cream (optional)

1. Preheat the oven to 350°F. Have you ever **cored** an apple? You'll need to core all six. Hold the apple on the cutting board, making sure you hold the sides of the apple, not the bottom. Push the corer into the top of the stem. See photo. My corer is kind of small, so I push it through three or four times to make a 1-inch hole. Put the cored apples in the greased baking dish.

2. Put the rest of the ingredients into the mixing bowl. Either mix it all together with the wooden spoon, or have fun and squish it together with your clean hands.

3. Fill the hollow apples with the oatmeal mixture. If you have extra of the mixture, pile it on top. Bake for 20 to 25 minutes.

4. Use your potholders to take the apples out of the oven, and let them cool before you eat them. I like to top each apple with a scoop of vanilla ice cream just before serving.

fork it over

Fruity-Tooty Salads

Of course, you know you can make fruit salad out of whatever fruits are in season and then just mix and match the dressings. Here are two of my favorite combos.

EQUIPMENT

colander • chef's knife • paring knife • cutting board • measuring cups and spoons • large mixing bowl • small bowl • fork • wooden spoon

The Bomb

- 1 apple, cored and diced
- 1 banana, peeled and sliced
- 1 cup strawberries, hulled and sliced
- handful of walnut pieces
- handful of raisins
- ¼ cup tahini
- ¼ cup maple syrup (My mama says to use real maple syrup, not maple-flavored syrup.)

Peachy Keen

- 3 peaches, washed, peeled, and sliced (Work over the mixing bowl when you peel, so the juice isn't lost.)
- 1 cup of blueberries, rinsed and picked
- ½ cup slivered almonds
- ½ teaspoon vanilla extract
- ¼ teaspoon powdered ginger
- 2 tablespoons honey

EACH RECIPE MAKES 3 TO 5 SERVINGS

1. Put the apple, banana, and strawberries in the mixing bowl along with the walnuts pieces and the raisins.

2. Stir the tahini and the maple syrup together in the small bowl with a fork.

3. Pour the dressing over the fruit, and mix with the wooden spoon until everything is evenly distributed.

1. Using the same equipment from The Bomb recipe, put the peaches, blueberries, and slivered almonds in the large mixing bowl.

2. Combine the vanilla extract, the powdered ginger, and the honey in the small bowl. Stir them with a fork until blended. Pour the dressing over the fruit, and stir with the wooden spoon to combine.

Oh, My! Omelet

When I was in high school I made an after-school omelet for a boy I had a crush on, and pretty soon he was my boyfriend. My dazzling wit and fabulous good looks may have had something to do with it, or maybe he just loved my omelet.

EQUIPMENT

small nonstick skillet • stove • mixing bowl • fork • chef's knife • cutting board • spatula (for flipping)

1 OMELET

- 2 eggs
- pinch of salt
- pinch of pepper
- a few drops of hot pepper sauce (optional)
- 1 tomato, diced
- handful of sprouts
- ¼ cup cream cheese (about 2 ounces)

Make Mmmushroom

Use sliced mushrooms, sliced or grated Swiss cheese, and rosemary as your filling.

Spintacular

Spinach, sliced or grated cheddar cheese, cream cheese, and a pinch of nutmeg make a spectacular omelet.

Sweet Stuff

Forget about the veggies and instead use cream cheese and your favorite jam to taste.

Appleicious

Combine sliced apple, sliced or grated cheddar cheese, and deli turkey as your filling.

1. Heat the nonstick skillet over medium heat. When it's hot enough to make a drop of water sizzle, it's hot enough to cook your eggs.

2. Crack the eggs into the mixing bowl. Add the salt, pepper, and hot pepper sauce, and beat with the fork. Pour the eggs into the skillet so they cover most of the pan. Let them cook undisturbed until the edges get solid.

3. After the edges are solid, scatter the tomato, sprouts, and cream cheese over one side (one half) of the cooked egg.

4. When the eggs are no longer runny, carefully slip the spatula under the half without the goodies. With one quick flip, fold the egg in half. See photo. Did you get it all in one piece? Congratulations! Did it tear? No biggie—it'll still taste great.

5. Turn off the stove, slide the omelet onto a plate, and enjoy.

fork it over

Double-Done Potatoes

I call these "double-done" because the potatoes cook twice. The surprising thing is, their deliciousness is actually quadrupled. You'll taste the proof in every bite, but you'll have to ask your algebra teacher for an equation that explains how it's possible.

EQUIPMENT

toaster oven (or oven) • chef's knife • cutting board • microwave (optional) • spoon • mixing bowl • baking sheet • sauce pot with lid • stove • slotted spoon • measuring cups and spoons • fork • potholders • grater

1 OR 2 SERVINGS

- 1 baked potato, halved
- 1 cup broccoli florets
- ¼ cup water
- ¼ cup sour cream
- crumbled bacon to taste (optional)
- chopped scallions to taste (optional)
- salt and pepper to taste
- 2 tablespoons grated cheddar cheese (about 2 ounces)

1. Turn the toaster oven to broil. Cut the baked potato in half lengthwise. (Don't have a leftover baked potato? Just wash, dry, and lightly oil a raw potato, and then cook it in a microwave for about 6 minutes. Then press the backside of a spoon onto the potato's center. If the potato doesn't easily "give," cook it for 2 to 6 more minutes. Let the potato cool before you cut it.)

2. Use the spoon to scoop the potato's insides into the bowl. Put the empty potato skins upside down on the baking sheet, and broil them for 7 minutes to make them crispy.

3. While the skins are crisping, put the broccoli florets and the water in the pot, cover the pot with the lid, and cook on the stovetop on medium heat for 7 minutes, or until the broccoli is bright green.

4. Add the sour cream to the potato innards, and mash with the fork. (Crumbled bacon or scallions—or both—make a tasty addition to the filling.) Add salt and pepper to taste, and use the slotted spoon to add the broccoli. Stir well.

5. Use your potholders to remove the skins from the oven and turn them right side-up. Spoon the filling into the skins. Sprinkle the cheese on top. Then broil for 7 minutes, or until the cheese melts and the filling is hot.

6. If you burn your tongue on the great food you've cooked, you won't be able to taste it. So make sure your Double-Done Potatoes are cool enough to eat before you dig in.

Terrific Tuna

Tuna salad isn't boring when you make it your way and stuff it into a tomato. My husband, Steve, adds all kinds of crazy stuff—capers, hot peppers, apples, cumin—whatever he finds in the kitchen. Feel free to experiment with your own flavor combinations.

EQUIPMENT

oven • paring knife • cutting board • spoon • measuring spoons • paper • towels • can opener • mixing bowl • baking dish • potholders

4 STUFFED TOMATOES

- 4 medium-sized tomatoes
- ½ teaspoon salt
- 6-ounce can of tuna packed in water, or 3-ounce pouch of tuna
- small onion, halved and diced (optional)
- ½ stalk of celery, diced
- 2 tablespoons pickle relish (Sweet or dill, you choose.)
- 2 tablespoons mayonnaise
- 2 tablespoons mustard
- 1 teaspoon dill
- salt and pepper to taste
- 2 teaspoons bread crumbs

1. Preheat the oven to 350°F. Carefully cut a 2-inch hole out of the stem end of each tomato with the paring knife. Scoop the seeds out of the tomatoes with the spoon. Sprinkle a pinch of salt in each tomato, and let them rest upside down on the paper towels while you make the tuna salad. See photo.

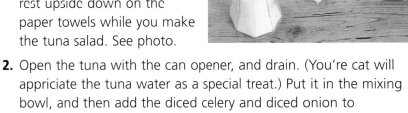

2. Open the tuna with the can opener, and drain. (You're cat will appriciate the tuna water as a special treat.) Put it in the mixing bowl, and then add the diced celery and diced onion to the bowl.

3. Add the relish, the mayonnaise, the mustard, and the dill. Stir it all up and then have a taste. Add just enough salt and pepper to make it perfect to your taste buds.

4. Fill the tomatoes with tuna salad, top with the bread crumbs, and put them in the baking dish. Bake for 15 to 20 minutes. (Remember to use potholders when taking the dish out of the oven.)

fork it over

Mac Attack

Who doesn't love mac & cheese? I guarantee this recipe is tastier than the kind from a box. Grating the onions adds flavor without messing up the texture.

3 TO 7 SERVINGS

- water
- 1 teaspoon salt
- 1 tablespoon vegetable oil
- 1½ cups dry macaroni
- 3 tablespoons butter
- ½ onion, grated
- 3 tablespoons flour
- 2 cups milk
- pinch of nutmeg
- 4 ounces Monterey Jack cheese, grated
- 4 ounces cheddar cheese, grated
- 4 ounces mozzarella cheese, grated
- cooking spray
- ¼ cup bread crumbs (optional)

1. Preheat the oven to 375°F. Fill the 4-quart pot halfway with water. Add the salt and oil, and bring to a boil over high heat.

2. Add the macaroni and boil over low heat. (The package directions will tell you exactly how long to let the macaroni cook. But you should reduce this time by 5 minutes, because it cooks more in the oven later.)

3. When the macaroni is cooked, turn off the stove. Use pot holders if needed to pour the cooked macaroni into the colander to drain. If the pot is too large for you to easily and safely handle, have an adult do this step.

4. Melt the butter in the sauce pot on medium heat. Then cook the onion in the butter for 2 to 3 minutes. Next, whisk the flour into the butter. This is called a **roux** (pronounced "roo"). See photo.

5. Gradually add the milk, whisking to break up as many lumps as you can. Cook the sauce, stirring occasionally with the whisk, until it thickens. It should take 5 to 8 minutes.

6. Stir the grated cheeses into the sauce with the whisk until the cheeses melt. Next, stir the macaroni into the cheesy sauce.

7. Dump the mac and cheese into the greased baking dish. Sprinkle the bread crumbs on top if you want to. Bake for 30 to 35 minutes. Use your potholders to take the baking dish out of the oven.

Puffy Apple Pancake

I thought I invented this recipe when I was 13. I loved pancakes, but they were too much work for a snack, so I figured out how to decrease the recipe and cook all of the batter at once. When I started writing this book I discovered other recipes for the exact same thing! I was kind of bummed out, but at least the world hasn't been deprived of puffy apple pancakes.

EQUIPMENT

vegetable peeler • apple corer (optional) • chef's knife • cutting board • whisk • measuring cups and spoons • mixing bowl • small nonstick skillet with lid • stove • spatula • potholders • sifter

1 GIANT PANCAKE

- 1 big green apple, peeled, cored, and diced (I recommend a Granny Smith apple.)
- $1/4$ teaspoon cinnamon
- 2 tablespoons sugar
- $1/3$ cup flour
- pinch of salt
- $1 1/2$ teaspoons baking powder
- 1 egg
- $1/2$ teaspoon vanilla
- $1/4$ cup milk
- 2 teaspoons butter
- powdered sugar

1. Whisk together the cinnamon, sugar, flour, salt, baking powder, egg, vanilla, and milk until combined, but don't worry about lumps. (This is one of those recipes with baking powder, so you need to measure carefully.)

2. Melt the butter in the skillet on medium heat. Add the apples, and then pour the batter over them. Cover the skillet with the lid and cook for 10 to 12 minutes.

3. Turn off the stove, take the skillet off the burner, and remove the lid.

4. Use the spatula to loosen the cake from the sides of the skillet. Next, put the serving plate upside-down over the skillet, and flip the pancake onto the plate by turning the whole thing over. (Use potholders to protect your hands).

5. Sift powdered sugar over the top (which used to be the bottom). Savor your masterpiece.

fork it over

Potato Volcano

Who says you can't play with your food? You'll use your hands to sculpt the mashed potatoes, and then scoop out a volcano crater to hold extra cheese sauce for tree—I mean broccoli—dunking. Just be sure to let the cheese cool first, or you'll suffer from lava-mouth.

EQUIPMENT

oven • chef's knife • cutting board • pot • stove • small sauce pot with lid • colander • measuring cups and spoons • masher • oven-safe serving plate • fork • mixing bowl • electric mixer • grater • spoon • potholders

3 DOOMED ISLANDS

- 6 red potatoes, chopped (about 3 cups)
- water
- 1 teaspoon salt
- 1 cup broccoli florets
- ¼ cup milk
- salt and pepper to taste
- ⅔ cup grated cheddar cheese
- ¼ cup whipping cream

1. Preheat the oven to 375°F. Put the potatoes chunks into the pot with the salt and enough water to cover them by at least three inches. Boil the potatoes for about 12 minutes, or until they're soft.

2. While the potatoes are boiling, steam the broccoli florets by putting ½ inch of water in the small pot with the broccoli. Cover the pot, and cook 7 minutes on medium-high heat.

3. Turn off the stove, and get an adult to drain the potatoes in the colander. Then dump the potatoes back into the pot, add the milk, and mash, mash, mash until you've gotten all of the lumps out that you can!

4. Taste the mashed potatoes. Add the salt and the pepper until the potatoes taste delicious to you. Remember, the cheese will boost the flavor of the finished dish. Then form the potatoes into a cone on the serving plate. Use the fork to make ridges, so it looks like a craggy mountain. Make a crater indentation at the top that looks like a little bowl.

5. Pour the whipping cream into the mixing bowl. Whip the cream with the electric mixer until it forms soft peaks. Stir in the cheese. Spoon the cream-and-cheese mixture into the volcano crater. Bake for 10 to 12 minutes, or until the cheesy lava is bubbling and oozing down the sides.

6. Remove the potato volcano from the oven (use your potholders), and decorate the base of the volcano with broccoli. Wait for the lava flow to cool before you devour this delicious disaster.

Noodle Kugel

3 TO 5 SERVINGS

If you're Jewish or have family from Eastern Europe, you may have had a savory version of kugel as a side dish. It's yummy, but this sweet kind is my favorite. It makes me feel cozy.

- water
- ½ teaspoon salt
- 4 ounces egg noodles
- 1 apple, grated
- 2 eggs
- ¼ cup raisins
- ⅓ cup sugar
- ¾ teaspoon cinnamon
- 2 tablespoons butter
- cooking spray
- 2 tablespoons bread crumbs

1. Preheat the oven to 375°F. Fill the pot halfway with the water. Add the salt, and bring to a boil on high heat.

2. Cook the noodles in the boiling water on low heat for 8 to 10 minutes. Turn off the stovetop when they are done.

3. While the noodles are cooking, crack the eggs into the mixing bowl and discard the shells. Then add the apple, raisins, sugar, and cinnamon. Use the spoon to combine the ingredients.

4. Use potholders to pour the pot of noodles into the colander to drain. Then return the drained noodles to the pot. If the pot is heavy or hard for you to handle, have an adult do the pouring.

5. Now quickly add the butter to the warm noodles, and stir with the wooden spoon until the butter melts. Add the apple mixture to the noodles and combine.

6. Transfer the noodle-apple concoction to the baking dish, and sprinkle the bread crumbs on top. Bake for 15 to 20 minutes. Use potholders to remove your Noodle Kugel from the oven, and let it cool before you serve it or try a bite.

fork it over

Cheery Cherry Crumble

Make sure you get cherries packed in juice for this recipe, not cherry pie filling. If you use the wrong ingredient you'll be disappointed with your Cheery Cherry Crumble, which would be ironic. If you like the "crumble" part best, double the ingredients for the topping.

EQUIPMENT

oven • can opener • measuring cups and spoons • mixing bowl • wooden spoon • greased baking dish • microwave • microwave-safe bowl • potholders • baking sheet (optional)

6 TO 8 SERVINGS

- 2 cans of cherries in juice, each can 14.5 ounces, drained
- 3 tablespoons corn starch
- 1¼ cup sugar
- ½ teaspoon vanilla extract
- pinch of salt

For the topping

- ¼ cup butter
- ⅓ cup flour
- ⅓ cup sugar

1. Preheat the oven to 350°F. Put the cherries, cornstarch, 1¼ cup sugar, vanilla, and salt in the mixing bowl. Stir with the wooden spoon to combine, and then dump the mixture into the greased baking dish. (You'll use the rest of the sugar in the crumble.)

2. Melt the butter in the microwave-safe bowl in the microwave for about 1 minute. Use the potholders when you take the bowl out of the microwave.

3. Add the flour and the ⅓ cup sugar to the melted butter. Stir with the wooden spoon to combine.

4. Use your fingers to crumble the topping over the cherries, and then bake for 45 for 50 minutes. (If the baking dish is really full, put a baking sheet under it when you put it in the oven. This is so it doesn't make a mess in your oven, which can be hard to clean.) Remember to use potholders when you take the dish out of the oven, and let the food cool before you dig in.

Now this is a treat: A whole chapter of eat-with-a-spoon snacks, beginning with one of my favorites.

Make this one-of-a-kind berry soup using vanilla soymilk or orange juice instead of milk, if you're not a milk fan. By the way, the berries in the picture came from my garden.

Berry Berry Bowl

EQUIPMENT

colander • chef's knife • cutting board • measuring cups and spoons • blender or food processor • serving bowls

2 TO 3 SERVINGS

- 1½ cups strawberries (about 8 big strawberries), washed and hulled
- ¾ cup milk
- 3 tablespoons sugar
- ⅔ cup blueberries, rinsed and picked
- ⅔ cup raspberries, rinsed and picked

1. Taste-test the berries. If they are super-sweet, use only 1 or 2 tablespoons of sugar in step 2.

2. Puree the strawberries, milk, and sugar in the blender.

3. Divide the blueberries and the raspberries between serving bowls. Pour the strawberry mixture over the berries in the bowls. Enjoy the taste of summer.

Chow-Down Chowder

I like my chowder with lots and lots of black pepper. But since not everyone likes it that way, I add the spice to my own bowl instead of to the whole pot.

6 TO 8 SERVINGS

- 8 plum-sized red potatoes, diced
- water
- 2 tablespoons butter
- 1 small white onion, peeled and diced
- 1 stalk of celery, diced
- ½ of a green pepper, diced
- 1 bay leaf
- ¼ cup flour
- 3 cups (or 1 pound) frozen corn
- 1½ teaspoons salt
- 1 cup milk
- pepper on the side

Low-Country Style

The area of the Atlantic coast around Charleston, South Carolina, is called the Low Country. They have fun beaches and delicious food, like this corn chowder variation: add 3 ounces of diced ham (about 3 slices worth) to the roux pot before melting the butter. Leave out the salt. (Country ham is salty.)

1. Put the potatoes in one of the pots, and add enough water to cover them, plus an extra 2 cups. Bring to a boil on high heat. Reduce the heat to medium, and boil 10 minutes, uncovered, until the potatoes are soft.

2. In the second pot, melt the butter on medium heat. Then sweat the onion, the celery, the green pepper, and the bay leaf in the melted butter for 3 for 5 minutes, or until you can almost see through the onions.

3. Sprinkle the flour over the onion mixture, and stir with the whisk. The goopy butter-flour mixture is called a **roux** (pronounced "roo"). See page 82 for a photo of roux.

4. Ladle some of the hot potato water (about 1 ½ cups, but you don't need to measure it exactly) into the roux pot. Stir with the whisk until most of it is smooth. (Of course, the veggies won't be smooth.)

5. Add the corn and the salt to the roux.

6. Mash the potatoes with the potato masher in the water they were cooked in until they're mush. Don't splash—it's hot! Then add the potato mush and the milk to the roux pot and bring it to a simmer while stirring occasionally.

7. Ladle the chowder into bowls. Season to taste with the pepper. Whoever gets the bay leaf gets to make a wish. But don't eat it! Bay leaf is about as tasty as shrimp tails.

lovin' every spoonful

Soba-licious

EQUIPMENT

measuring cups and spoons • sauce pot • stove • skillet • chef's knife • cutting board • spatula • small bowl (optional, to soak arame) • vegetable peeler • bar zester (optional) • tongs • 2 or 3 serving bowls • ladle

Once upon a time I ate this almost every day for a year. It's that good. You can find soba noodles and arame seaweed with the Asian foods at the grocery store. And you can always use linguini if you don't have soba noodles.

2 TO 3 SERVINGS

- 3 cups water
- 1 tablespoon soy sauce
- 3 ounces soba noodles (1 bundle that's about 1 inch in diameter)
- 1 tablespoon vegetable oil
- 1/8 teaspoon red pepper flakes
- 4 ounces firm tofu, diced into 1/2-inch cubes
- 2 tablespoons arame seaweed, soaked in water according to package instructions (It's optional, but I highly recommend you give arame a try.)
- 1 scallion, washed and sliced
- 1/2 peeled carrot, then made into thin strips with a bar zester or vegetable peeler
- 1/4 teaspoon powdered ginger
- 1/2 teaspoon sugar
- 1/2 teaspoon rice vinegar
- 1/2 teaspoon sesame oil

1. Bring the water and the soy sauce to a boil in the sauce pot over high heat. Add the noodles, and cook for 10 to 12 minutes on low heat.

2. Heat the vegetable oil and the red pepper flakes in the skillet on medium-high heat. You'll know it's hot enough to begin cooking if the water sizzles when you flick a drop in the pan.

3. Brown the tofu by sautéing it for 3 to 5 minutes while stirring occasionally.

4. Use tongs to divide the noodles between the two serving bowls. Save the cooking water.

5. Divide the arame, tofu, scallions, and carrot strips between the two bowls.

6. Add the ginger, sugar, rice vinegar, and sesame oil to the noodle water, and ladle it into the bowls. I eat the noodles with chopsticks and the broth with a spoon.

Broc-n-Roll

3 TO 5 SERVINGS

My friend Chuck grows lots of broccoli in his garden, which is a good thing because he's crazy about this soup. The first time he made it he couldn't believe how easy it was! You can make this recipe with cauliflower instead of broccoli, or try using half of each.

- 1 medium head of broccoli cut into 1½-inch chunks (stems, too)
- 2 cups diced potatoes
- 2 cloves peeled garlic
- 1 quart chicken or vegetable broth
- 1 teaspoon salt
- ½ teaspoon pepper
- ¼ teaspoon nutmeg
- 1 cup whole milk, or ¾ cup half and half
- cheddar cheese, grated (optional)

1. Put the broccoli, potatoes, garlic, and chicken broth into the sauce pot, and bring to a boil on high heat. When the soup boils, reduce the heat to medium, and cook 10 to 12 minutes until the vegetables are soft.

2. Use the slotted spoon to transfer the broccoli and garlic to the blender. Purée the ingredients.

3. Add the pureed broccoli mixture back to the broth, and bring the soup back to a simmer.

4. Stir in the salt, pepper, nutmeg, and milk. Don't boil the soup after the milk has been added. Just heat it to a good eating temperature. If you want, sprinkle some cheddar onto each bowl of soup.

lovin' every spoonful

Gaz-whatcho?

It's called gazpacho, and it's a refreshing snack on a hot day. You'll notice I didn't put exact measurements for everything. That's because it all really depends on the tomatoes. Fresh-from-the-garden tomatoes probably don't need any vinegar and sugar. Grocery store tomatoes can often use a little help in the flavor department.

EQUIPMENT

chef's knife • cutting board • vegetable peeler • measuring cups and spoons • blender or food processor • spoon

2 TO 4 SERVINGS

- 2 tomatoes, chopped (Don't forget to remove the stem area.)
- ½ cucumber, peeled, seeded, and chopped (Use the spoon to scrape out the seeds. See page 70.)
- ¼ onion, peeled and chopped
- ½ green pepper
- ½ cup cilantro
- 1 tablespoon olive oil
- ½ teaspoon salt
- ⅛ teaspoon pepper
- ¼ to 2 tablespoons vinegar (optional)
- ¼ to 2 teaspoon sugar (optional)

1. Prepare the green pepper for chopping by first halving it by cutting it from stem to end. Then use one hand to pull out the seeds, the white membrane you see, and the stem. See photo. Discard them and then chop up the pepper.

2. Put the tomatoes, cucumber, onion, and green pepper into the blender. Add the cilantro, olive oil, salt, and pepper. Put the top on the blender, and puree until smooth.

3. Taste a spoonful, and adjust the thickness and flavor with water, vinegar, and/or sugar. Puree briefly to combine the additional flavorings, if necessary. Pour each serving into a bowl.

Great Pumpkin Soup

Pumpkin isn't just for pie, you know. It's also great in this savory soup. Make cool designs on the surface by pulling a wooden skewer or the tip of a knife through the yogurt. I wonder how it would look if you used a fork?

EQUIPMENT

sauce pot • stove • grater • wooden spoon • can opener • measuring cups and spoons • kitchen shears (optional)

3 OR 4 SERVINGS

- 1 tablespoon olive oil
- ½ onion, halved and grated
- 1 bay leaf
- 16-ounce can (or about 1½ cups) pumpkin purée (Make sure it's just pumpkin, not pumpkin pie filling.)
- 1½ cups chicken or veggie broth
- ¼ teaspoon paprika
- ⅛ teaspoon ground nutmeg
- ¾ teaspoon salt
- ⅛ teaspoon pepper
- 3 tablespoons plain or vanilla yogurt
- chives (optional)

1. Heat the olive oil in the sauce pot on medium-high heat. You'll know it's hot enough to cook in if you flick a drop of water into the pot and the water sizzles.

2. Sauté the onion and the bay leaf in the pot for 2 to 3 minutes, stirring occasionally with the wooden spoon, until you can almost see through the onion.

3. Add the pumpkin to the pot. Pour some broth into the pumpkin can, and then swirl it to get all the extra bits of pumpkin before adding the broth to the pot.

4. Add the paprika, nutmeg, salt, and pepper. Stir it all together and simmer for 5 to 10 minutes.

5. To serve, swirl a tablespoon of yogurt in each bowl, and, if you want, use the kitchen shears to snip chives onto the top.

lovin' every spoonful

Ooey Gooey

E Q U I P M E N T

toaster oven or oven • table knife •
measuring spoons • aluminum
foil • potholders

1 SERVING

OK, so stuffing marshmallows and peanut butter (especially the peanut butter) into a banana sounds a little weird. But don't let that stop you. If you haven't ever tried it, you really don't know what you're missing.

- 1 banana
- 2 tablespoons peanut butter
- 10 minimarshmallows
- a handful of chocolate chips

1. Preheat the toaster oven to 350°F. Peel a section of banana peel, but leave it attached at the end. See photo.

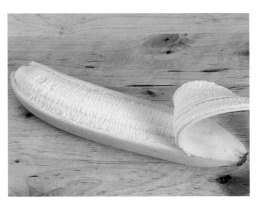

2. Use the table knife to cut a slot along the length of the banana. Fill the slot with the peanut butter, chocolate chips, and marshmallows.

3. Close the peel, and wrap the banana in the aluminum foil. Bake for 15 minutes.

4. Use the potholders when you take the banana out of the oven, and let the banana cool until you can unwrap it without burning yourself. Let your ooey-gooey banana cool before spooning in.

Cozy Cocoa Rice Pudding

When I was a kid, I had some friends from Italy whose dad traveled a lot for his job. When he was gone, they got to have a sort of chocolate, milk, and rice dish for dinner. I think their mom gave them that special treat so they wouldn't be so sad about their dad being gone. This recipe is my take on that treat.

EQUIPMENT

oven • wooden spoon • measuring cups and spoons • mixing bowl • whisk • greased baking dish or **ramekins** • potholders

6 TO 8 SERVINGS

- ¼ cup cocoa powder
- ½ cup brown sugar
- ⅛ teaspoon salt
- 1¼ cups milk
- ½ teaspoon vanilla
- 3 eggs
- 2 cups cooked rice (Use leftovers, or follow the package directions.)
- ½ cup dried cranberries (optional)

1. Preheat the oven to 350°F. Use the wooden spoon to combine the cocoa powder, brown sugar, and salt in the mixing bowl.

2. Add a splash or two of the milk (about ¼ cup, but you don't need to measure). Whisk until smooth.

3. Crack the eggs into the mixing bowl and discard the shells. Add the vanilla and the rest of the milk to the bowl. Whisk to combine. Then stir the rice and the cherries into the mixture with a wooden spoon.

4. Transfer the pudding to the baking dish or ramekins. Bake for 30 to 45 minutes. Smaller dishes bake faster.

5. Use your potholders to take the dish out of the oven. The middle should still jiggle a little if you shake the dish; it will firm up as it cools. Let it cool for 5 minutes before eating.

lovin' every spoonful

equipment glossary

Serrated knife

Vegetable peeler

Corer

Chef's knife

Bar zester

Paring knife

Measuring spoons

Kitchen shears

Liquid measuring cup

Scoop measuring cups

Ladle

Potato masher

Whisk

Rubber spatulas

Tongs

Spatula

Wooden spoons

Cutting boards

Grater

Strainer

Colander

Baking dish

Mixing bowls

Pots

Skillet

Food processor

Blender

Electric mixer

equipment glossary

glossary

Bake: heat comes from the bottom of the oven and evenly cooks food. See page 14.

Beat: stir kind of fast with a fork, electric mixer, or whisk until well combined and a little bit fluffy

Blend: use a blender

Boil: what happens to a liquid when it gets hot enough to evaporate—there are lots of big bubbles. See page 15.

Broil: high heat comes from the top of the oven to quickly melt cheese or brown the top of food. See page 14.

Brown: cooking meat or tofu in a skillet until it gets brown. See page 14 for a how-to photo.

Cage-free chickens: see Free-range chickens

Chopping: cutting food into pieces close to the same size: sloppy dicing. See page 13.

Chunks: big (about 1½ inches square) pieces of chopped food–they don't have to be perfect

Combine: stir together until evenly mixed. See page 11.

Core: using a corer to remove the tough middle section and seeds from apples or pears. See page 73 for a how-to photo.

Dicing: cutting food into cubes about half an inch on each side. See page 13.

Drain: pour the juice out of canned food; you can use a strainer, or hold the lid of the can against the food while you pour

Dredge: coating a piece of food in flour or a sea-soning mixture. See page 43 for a how-to photo.

Equipment: tools

Free-range chickens: chickens that get to peck around in a big pen or yard instead of being cooped up in a tiny cage all the time

Grating: using a grater to shred food. See page 13 for a how-to photo.

Greased: sprayed lightly with cooking spray or rubbed lightly with cooking oil so your food doesn't stick

Halving: cutting something into two equal pieces. See page 13 for a how-to photo.

Hull: removing the leaves and stems from straw-berries with your fingers or the tip of a spoon.

Ingredients: the different foods that go in a recipe

Microwave: cooking something in a microwave. Follow the manufacturer's instructions.

Mincing: cutting food into tiny pieces. See page 13 for a how-to photo.

Non-dominant hand: the hand that you don't write with

Nonstick: a type of skillet or pan with an interior coating that prevents food from sticking. Don't use sharp utensils with nonstick equipment; it damages the coating. If the coating flakes off, don't use that pan anymore.

Pick: removing stems and bad berries.

Produce: fresh fruits and vegetables

Pulse: a setting on blenders and food processors that lets you turn them on and off in short bursts. See page 11.

Purée: a setting on blenders and food processors

that lets you make food soupy. See page 13.

Ramekins: baking dishes sized for individual servings. See examples in the recipe photos on pages 88 and 106.

Recipe: a plan for cooking up scrumptious snacks

Roux (pronounced "roo")**:** a mixture of melted butter and flour that thickens soups. See page 82 for a how-to photo.

Sauté: cooking food in a skillet over medium-high heat, stirring or flipping to cook the food on all sides. See page 14 for a how-to photo.

Simmer: cooking liquid at just below a boil—there are some small bubbles. See page 15 for a how-to photo.

Slicing: cutting food into thin, flat pieces. See page 13 for a how-to photo.

Strain: use a strainer or colander (depending on how big the pieces of food are) to separate solids from liquids

Sweat: cooking veggies (usually onions) in a skillet to make them release their juices. See page 14 for a how-to photo.

Toaster oven: a miniature oven, perfect for cooking snacks

Toss: use your clean hands or tongs to coat large pieces of food with sauce or spices. See page 11.

Utensils: small tools with handles

Whisk: the name of a tool, and the action of using it; whisking uses a wrist motion to beat and/or smooth out lumps

Acknowledgments

Thank you to the models, many of whom gave up the final day of summer vacation to work with us: Twana, Sarah, Marcus, Liz, Kia, Joseph, Ingrid, India, Eva, Daniel, Chelsea, Ben, and Alex.

To the parents and families of our models: thank you for everything you've done to raise great kids! Thank you also for making it possible for us to feature your sons and daughters in this book.

Special thanks go to Ben and Cate Scales and family for allowing us to use their beautiful home for all of the on-location photography.

Thanks to Lilly for the fabulous grocery list.

Index

Metrics

Need to convert the measurements in this book to metrics? Here's how:

To convert degrees Fahrenheit to degrees Celsius, subtract 32 and then multiply by .56.

To convert inches to centimeters, multiply by 2.5.

To convert ounces to grams, multiply by 28.

T convert teaspoons to milliliters, multiply by 5.

To convert tablespoons to milliliters, multiply by 15.

To convert cups to liters, multiply by .24.